Rhinoceros

ANIMALS That Make a Difference!

Lucy Bashford

Explore other books at:
WWW.ENGAGEBOOKS.COM

VANCOUVER, B.C.

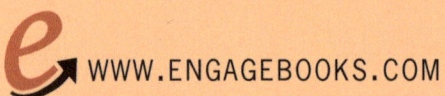 WWW.ENGAGEBOOKS.COM

Rhinoceros: Level 3
Animals That Make a Difference!
Bashford, Lucy, 1958
Text © 2024 Engage Books
Design © 2024 Engage Books

Edited by: A.R. Roumanis,
Sarah Harvey, Melody Sun, and Ashley Lee
Design by: Mandy Christiansen

Text set in Arial Regular.
Chapter headings set in Nathaniel-19.

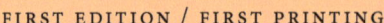

FIRST EDITION / FIRST PRINTING

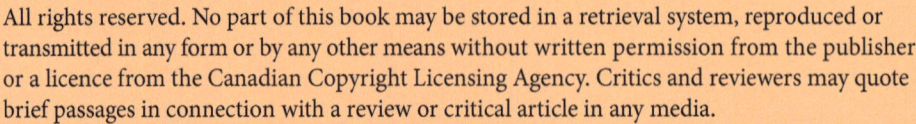

All rights reserved. No part of this book may be stored in a retrieval system, reproduced or transmitted in any form or by any other means without written permission from the publisher or a licence from the Canadian Copyright Licensing Agency. Critics and reviewers may quote brief passages in connection with a review or critical article in any media.

Every reasonable effort has been made to contact the copyright holders of all material reproduced in this book.

LIBRARY AND ARCHIVES CANADA CATALOGUING IN PUBLICATION

Title: Rhinoceros / Lucy Bashford.
Names: Bashford, Lucy, author.
Description: Series statement: Animals that make a difference

Identifiers: Canadiana (print) 20230448593 | Canadiana (ebook) 20230448607
ISBN 978-1-77476-828-0 (hardcover)
ISBN 978-1-77476-829-7 (softcover)
ISBN 978-1-77476-830-3 (epub)
ISBN 978-1-77476-831-0 (pdf)
ISBN 978-1-77878-138-4 (audio)

Subjects:
LCSH: Rhinoceroses—Juvenile literature.
LCSH: Human-animal relationships—Juvenile literature.

Classification: LCC QL737.U63 B38 2024 | DDC J599.66/8—DC23

This project has been made possible in part by the Government of Canada.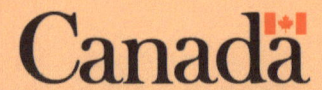

Contents

- 4   What Are Rhinoceros?
- 6   A Closer Look
- 8   Where Do Rhinoceros Live?
- 10   What Do Rhinoceros Eat?
- 12   How Do Rhinoceros Talk to Each Other?
- 14   Rhinoceros Life Cycle
- 16   Curious Facts About Rhinoceros
- 18   Kinds of Rhinoceros
- 20   How Rhinoceros Help Earth
- 22   How Rhinoceros Help Other Animals
- 24   How Rhinoceros Help Humans
- 26   Rhinoceros in Danger
- 28   How to Help Rhinoceros
- 30   Quiz

What Are Rhinoceros?

Rhinoceros are some of the largest living land **mammals**. They are also called rhinos. They have been on Earth for about 50 million years.

KEY WORD

Mammals: animals with warm blood and bones in their backs.

Most rhinoceros live alone. Only one **species** lives in groups. A group of rhinos is called a crash.

KEY WORD

Species: a group of similar animals or plants that can make babies with each other.

A Closer Look

Rhinos are often brown, gray, or black. Most rhinos weigh between 1,765 and 5,511 pounds (800 to 2,500 kilograms). They can grow to be 8 to 13 feet (2.5 to 4 meters) long.

Rhino skin gets sunburned easily. They roll in mud or dust to protect their skin.

Rhinos can have one or two horns. Some rhinos use their horns to protect themselves.

Rhinos have three toes on each foot. The tip of each toe is covered in a hard nail.

Where Do Rhinoceros Live?

Rhinos live in grasslands, forests, or deserts. Most rhinos live in **wildlife reserves** or national parks. Very few rhinos live outside of these areas.

KEY WORD

Wildlife reserves: areas of land that are protected so plants and animals can be kept safe.

Rhinos live in Africa and Asia. The Javan rhino is only found on the island of Java. Sumatran rhinos live on the islands of Sumatra and Borneo. African rhinos are found in just four African countries. These are South Africa, Namibia, Zimbabwe, and Kenya.

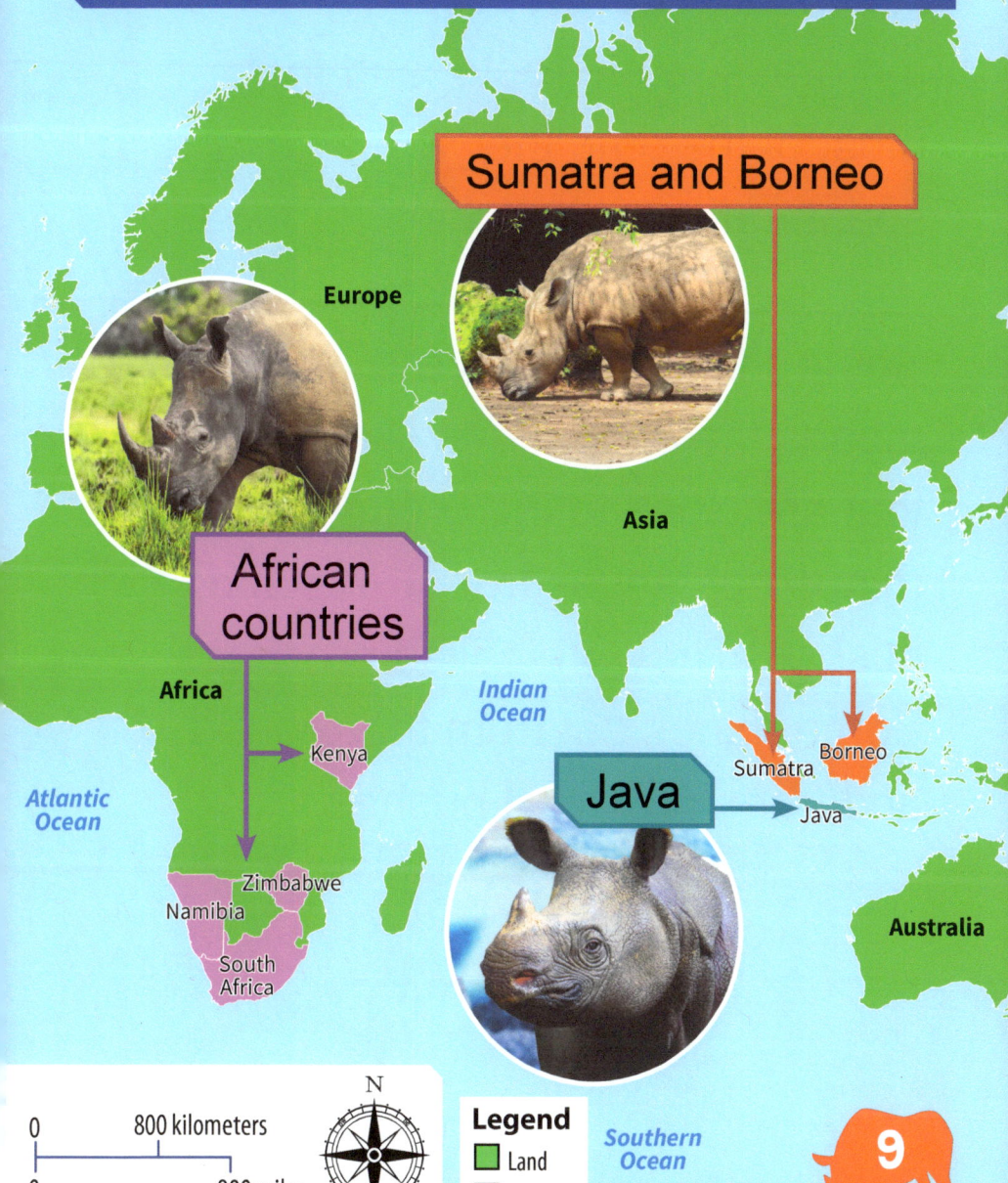

What Do Rhinoceros Eat?

Rhinos are **herbivores**. They eat grass, bark, roots, and fruit. Most of the time they are awake is spent eating and looking for food.

Some rhinos are grazers. This means they eat plants like grass that are close to the ground. Other rhinos eat leaves from trees and bushes. They are called browsers. Some rhinos eat from the ground and from trees and bushes.

KEY WORD

Herbivores: animals that eat only plants.

Large rhinos can eat about 110 lbs (50 kgs) of food every day.

11

How Do Rhinoceros Talk to Each Other?

Rhinos make many sounds. When they are happy, they moo or whine. They might growl or snort if they are angry. Mothers use special sounds to call their babies.

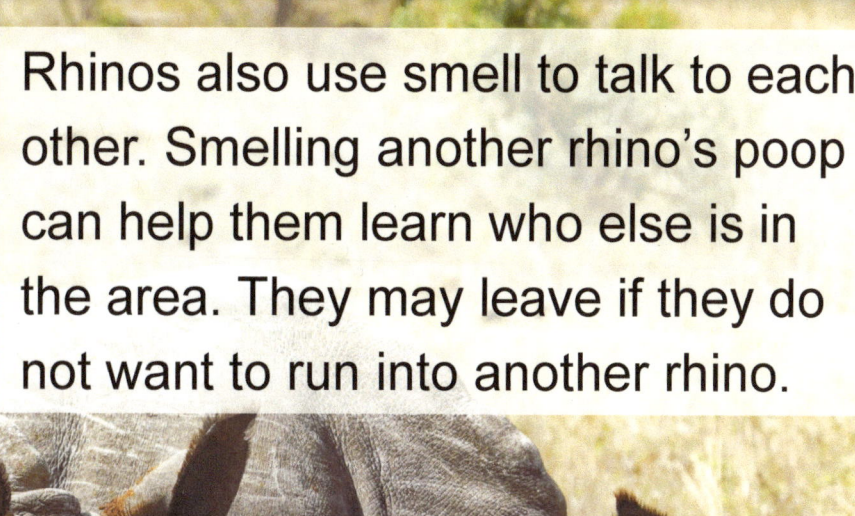

Rhinos also use smell to talk to each other. Smelling another rhino's poop can help them learn who else is in the area. They may leave if they do not want to run into another rhino.

Rhinos will often poop in the same area as others to create a kind of message board for other rhinos passing through.

Rhinoceros Life Cycle

Female rhinos have a baby every two to five years. They are pregnant for about 16 months. They usually only have one baby at a time.

Baby rhinos are called calves. They can stand a few hours after birth. It takes a few days before they are able to walk properly.

Calves are born without horns. Their horns start to grow after a few months. They continue to grow for the rest of a rhino's life.

Calves stay with their mothers until they are about two to four years old. Then they go live on their own. Rhinos live for about 35 to 45 years in the wild.

Curious Facts About Rhinoceros

Asian rhinos are great swimmers, but African rhinos are not.

Rhinos can run up to 30 miles (45 kilometers) per hour.

Most rhinos only have hair on their ears and tails. The Sumatran rhino is the only rhino with hair on its body.

Rhinos cannot see very well. They will sometimes charge at a rock if they think it is another rhino.

A rhino's horn will grow back if it breaks.

The name rhinoceros comes from the Greek language. Rhino means "nose," and ceros means "horn."

Kinds of Rhinoceros

There are five kinds of rhinoceros. The two African rhinos are called the black rhino and the white rhino.

The black rhino and the white rhino are actually the same gray color.

The white rhino is the largest of all rhinos. They live in groups.

The three Asian rhinos are called the Sumatran rhino, the Javan rhino, and the greater one-horned rhino.

Javan rhinos and greater one-horned rhinos have one horn. All other rhinos have two horns.

How Rhinoceros Help Earth

Rhinos choose to eat some plants over others. This allows these other plants to grow. Having lots of different plants in an area helps keep **ecosystems** healthy.

KEY WORD

Ecosystems: communities of living and nonliving things that work together to stay healthy.

Rhinos eat a lot of seeds when they eat plants. These seeds come out in their poop. The rhino poop helps them grow into plants. Rhinos help these seeds travel farther than they would be able to on their own.

How Rhinoceros Help Other Animals

Rhinos often get covered in bugs like ticks. Birds called oxpeckers like to sit on rhinos' backs and eat these bugs. This helps both the oxpeckers and rhinos.

Rhinos like to **wallow** in mud puddles or rivers. When they do this, their big bodies help keep water holes open. They will sometimes dig in the soil to find water hidden beneath it. This gives other animals places to drink.

KEY WORD

Wallow: roll or lie in mud or water to stay cool or keep bugs away.

Oxpeckers can see better than rhinos and will often warn rhinos of danger rhinos cannot see.

How Rhinoceros Help Humans

People who live near rhinos eat the plants rhinos help grow. These plants also soak up harmful gases from the air. This makes the air people breathe cleaner.

Many people travel to Africa and Asia just to see rhinos. This helps create new jobs for local people. It also helps local businesses bring in money.

Rhinoceros in Danger

Rhinos are one of the world's most **endangered** animals. In the early 1900s, there were over 500,000 rhinos. Today there are only about 27,000 rhinos in the wild.

KEY WORD
Endangered: at risk of dying out forever.

One of the biggest threats to rhinos is **poachers**. They kill rhinos so they can take and sell their horns. Some people believe rhino horns can cure illnesses. This is not true.

KEY WORD

Poachers: people who hunt and kill animals that are protected by laws.

How to Help Rhinoceros

Learn all you can about rhinos. Share what you learn with others. The more people who know about rhinos and the problems they face, the more people there are to help them.

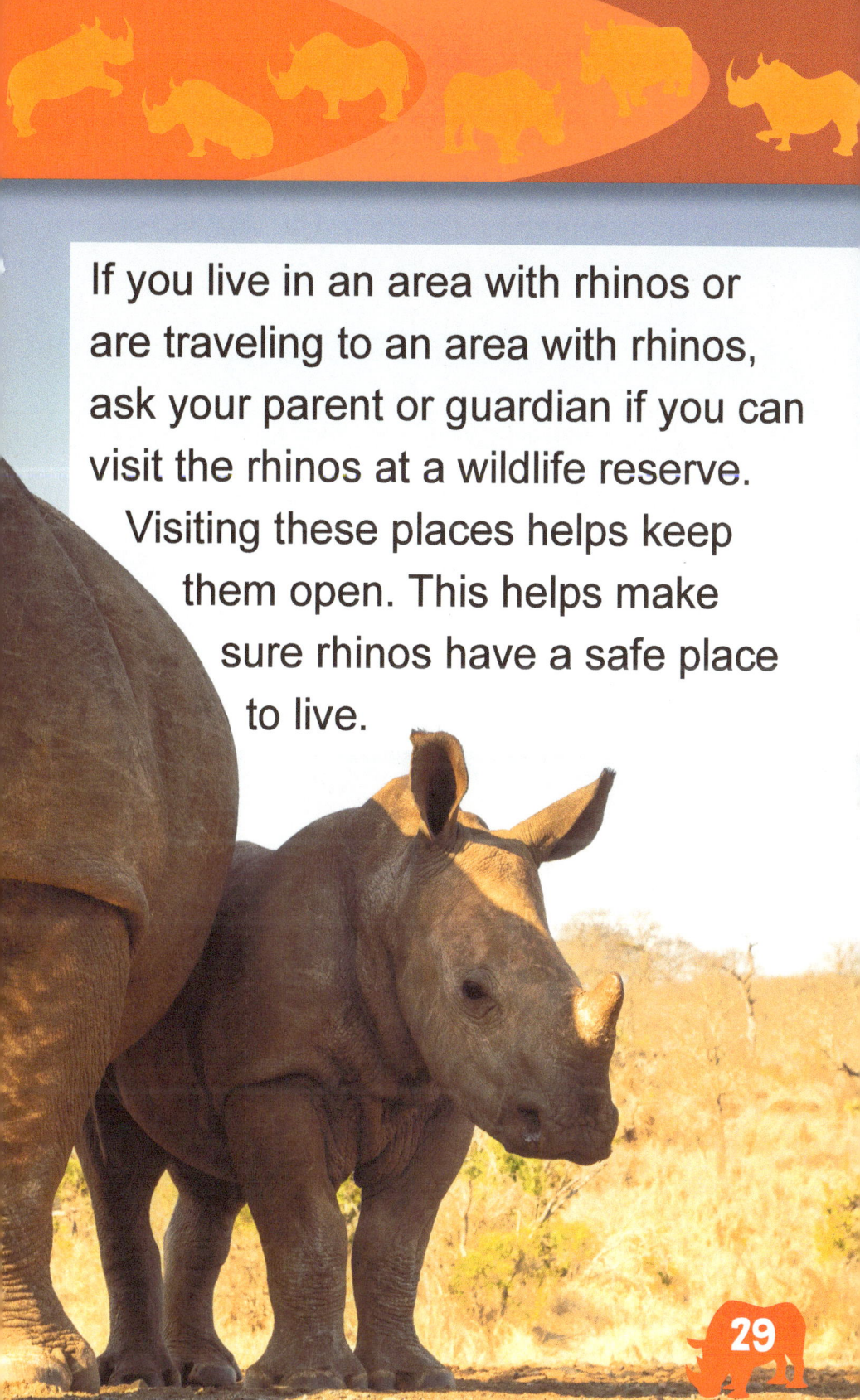

If you live in an area with rhinos or are traveling to an area with rhinos, ask your parent or guardian if you can visit the rhinos at a wildlife reserve. Visiting these places helps keep them open. This helps make sure rhinos have a safe place to live.

Quiz

Test your knowledge of rhinos by answering the following questions. The questions are based on what you have read in this book. The answers are listed on the bottom of the next page.

1 How long have rhinos been on Earth?

2 What do rhinos eat?

3 What are baby rhinos called?

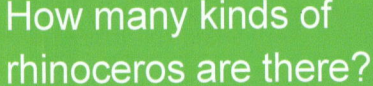

4 How many kinds of rhinoceros are there?

5 What is the name of the bird that likes to sit on rhinos' backs and eat bugs?

6 What is one of the biggest threats to rhinos?

Explore other books in the Animals That Make a Difference series

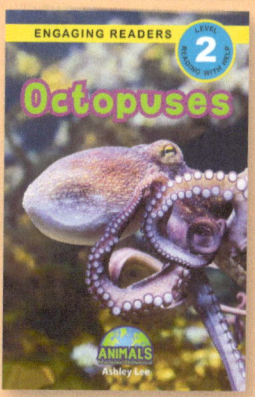
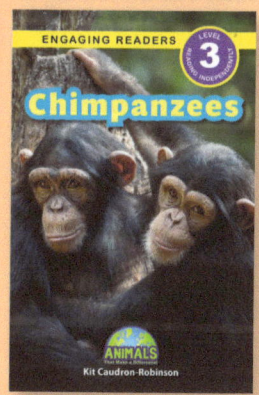
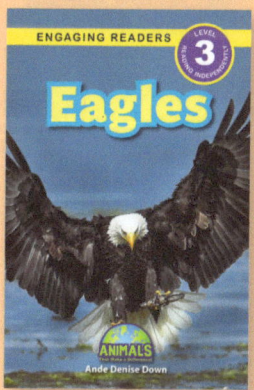
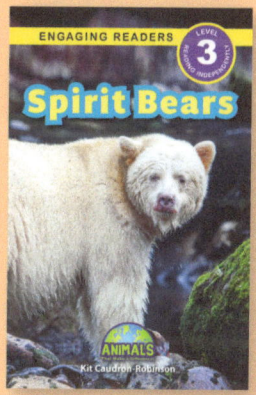

Visit www.engagebooks.com to explore more Engaging Readers.

Answers: 1. About 50 million years 2. Grass, bark, roots, and fruit 3. Calves 4. Five 5. Oxpecker 6. Poachers

Milton Keynes UK
Ingram Content Group UK Ltd.
UKHW051902300524
443359UK00001B/5